Mimic Makers

Biomimicry Inventors Inspired by Nature

Kristen Nordstrom

Illustrated by Paul Boston

Charlesbridge

Why do maple seeds twirl when they fall?

How does a gecko walk on walls?

Mimic makers wonder how nature works. They learn from living things such as animals, plants, and fungi. They mimic, or copy, good ideas to create useful inventions.

What can you learn from the living world? What can you invent? Be inspired by these mimic makers!

A Bullet Train with a Beak

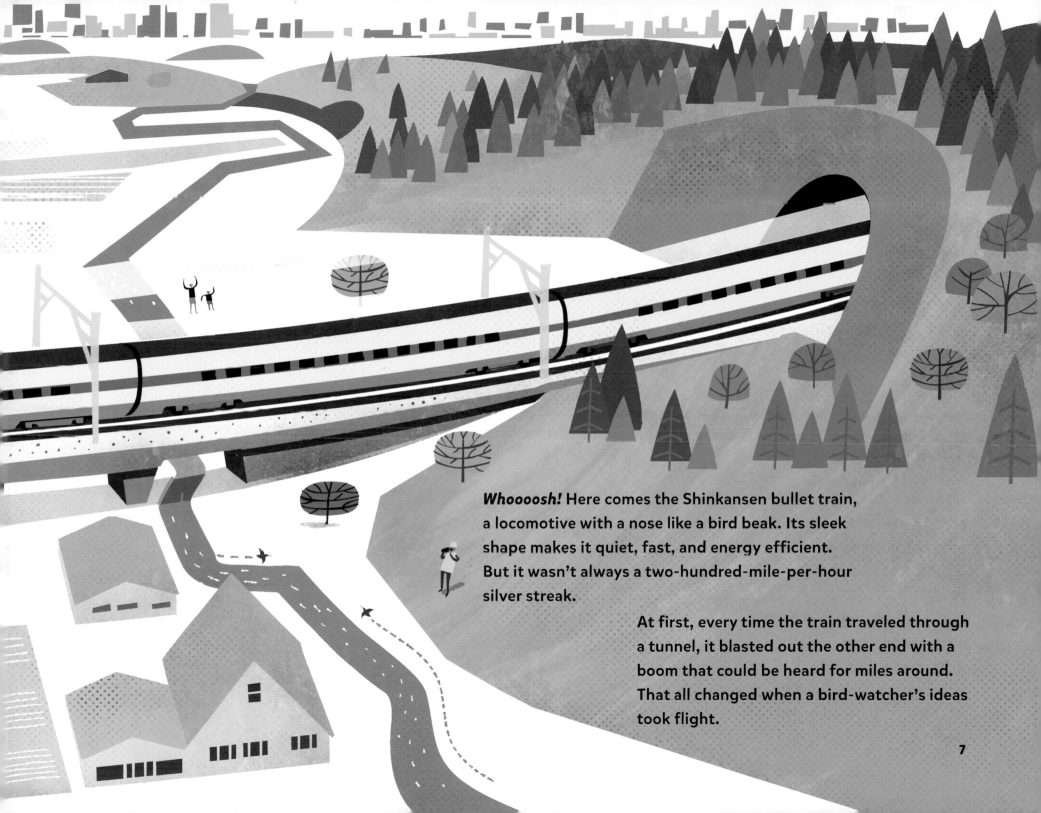

Whooooosh! Here comes the Shinkansen bullet train, a locomotive with a nose like a bird beak. Its sleek shape makes it quiet, fast, and energy efficient. But it wasn't always a two-hundred-mile-per-hour silver streak.

At first, every time the train traveled through a tunnel, it blasted out the other end with a boom that could be heard for miles around. That all changed when a bird-watcher's ideas took flight.

7

NAKATSU EIJI watched a kingfisher plunge like an arrow into the water below. How did this daring diver hit the surface with hardly a ripple? Eiji discovered that the kingfisher's pointed beak cuts smoothly through air and water.

Eiji brought this idea to work, where he was trying to redesign the Shinkansen. He shaped the nose of the train like the kingfisher's bill. This design streamlined the booming train into a quiet ride that "flies" faster and uses less energy.

Leaves Light Up

This shiny solar cell has superpowers. Like all solar cells, it soaks up sunlight and makes electricity. But this cell isn't flat and stiff like a solar panel on the roof of a house. It flexes and bends, and it's lightweight. It also absorbs more light than a flat solar cell of the same size. That's because it's designed after the best natural sun-catcher on the planet: the leaf. Who came up with this lovely, leafy idea?

YUEH-LIN (LYNN) LOO looked at a leaf under a microscope and saw shallow wrinkles and deep folds. Why was it so crinkly? Working with her team, Lynn discovered that the leaf's wrinkles and folds do two things: they soak up sunshine, and they channel light like a river channels water. This helps more light get absorbed. The more sunlight a plant absorbs, the more food it can make through photosynthesis.

12

Lynn decided to mimic this genius design to create a better solar cell. Her team invented a plastic sheet with wrinkles and folds like a leaf's surface. The sheet sticks to the surface of a bendable solar cell, and waves of sunlight flow through the wrinkles like water running through a hose. Lynn hopes that someday these solar cells will bring clean energy to people all over the world.

No Showers for Sharks

Sharklet is a thin film that can keep everything from ships to submarines spotless. A layer of this material can also stop germs from growing on medical devices, cell-phone cases, and other things we use every day.

Sharklet's secret is its super-tiny bumps and raised ridges, which repel algae and germs without the use of chemicals. This new technology was inspired by a fish that's been around since the time of the dinosaurs.

TONY BRENNAN watched a nuclear submarine rise to the surface of the sea. It was as long as seven school buses and covered with goopy green algae. Only hours of scrubbing and gallons of water would make this vessel shine again. Tony knew there must be a better way. That's when an idea swam right into his head. Sharks! These fish swim day and night in ocean water. How do they stay so clean?

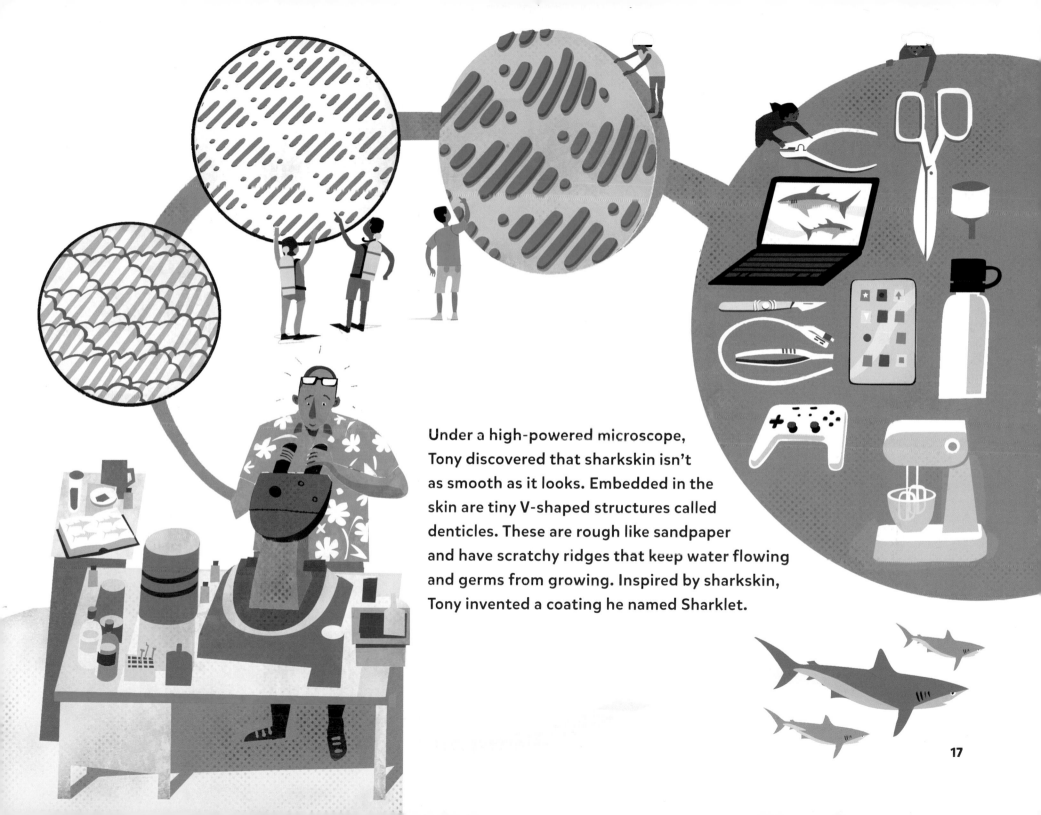

Under a high-powered microscope, Tony discovered that sharkskin isn't as smooth as it looks. Embedded in the skin are tiny V-shaped structures called denticles. These are rough like sandpaper and have scratchy ridges that keep water flowing and germs from growing. Inspired by sharkskin, Tony invented a coating he named Sharklet.

17

Drink Like a Bug

The Dew Bank bottle collects drinking water
from the morning mist. At night, this steel bottle
is put outside to cool. In the morning, when the
sun comes up, warm air hits the cold bottle.

The water in the air condenses and forms dew, which sticks to the bottle's outside bumps.

When the water droplets get heavy enough, they roll along channels to a holding chamber. Ah, sweet H_2O!

PAK KITAE was twelve years old when he saw a nature documentary about a Namibian beetle. He watched in wonder as the insect tipped its rear end up to the sky and collected water from the morning fog. This critter had found an amazing way to drink in the desert.

Twenty years later, the memory of this insect came buzzing back to Kitae. He remembered how water stuck to bumps on the beetle's back, then rolled in rivers into its mouth. Kitae decided to copy the beetle's shape to invent a water collector. He didn't need to come up with the perfect design. Nature had already done that.

A Friendly Fungus Among Us

This rice is doing the seemingly impossible. It's growing in hot, dry, salty soil. How does it survive?

If you zoom in close with a microscope, you'll see a fungus living inside the rice plant. This fungus keeps the rice growing strong. But it wasn't always there.

RODRIGUEZ and REDMAN

It all started with a fight over a plant. Panic grass grows near the boiling geothermal pools of Yellowstone National Park. Botanists, scientists who study plants, were sure the grass had changed to survive the heat. But two microbiologists disagreed. Rusty Rodriguez and Regina Redman study tiny organisms too small to see with the human eye. They had a hunch there was more to the mystery.

After years of research in the Wyoming wilderness, they discovered that the grass survives because it has a fungus living inside it. The grass and fungus have formed a symbiotic relationship, which is like a good friendship. The "buddies" help protect each other from the heat.

Rusty and Regina borrowed this idea to invent BioEnsure, a liquid containing the fungus. Seeds treated with BioEnsure can grow in harsh conditions without harmful chemicals, thanks to a friendly fungus.

From Fins to Fans

The bumpy blades on this turbine help make clean energy. As wind blows on the blades, the turbine spins and turns the wind's energy into electricity. This electricity helps keep lights on, refrigerators cool, and computers up and running.

The blades may be bumpy, but they're smooth operators. They're quieter and more efficient than straight blades. Some studies even show they put out more power. So how did these blades get their bumps?

27

FRANK FISH stood in an art gallery, staring at a sculpture of a humpback whale.

Something seemed wrong. He ran his finger over the curves of a flipper. He asked the gallery owner why the artist had made the front so lumpy.

28

The owner showed him a picture of a real humpback whale. To Frank's surprise, the leading edge of the flipper curved up and down in an uneven pattern of bumps. But why?

Frank discovered that the curvy shape helps move water evenly over the flipper. This enables a big whale to make tight turns. Frank wondered if he could design a turbine blade based on the same idea. After many tries, he invented a big, beautiful blade that moves through air just like a whale flipper moves through water.

Whirlybirds and Flying Machines

Stand back! A Samarai air vehicle is coming in for a landing. The single wing of this flying machine was modeled after the marvelous maple seed—with a few special additions. There's a thruster at its tip and a flap behind its wing. These extras help it hover in place. Who invented this fantastic flyer?

31

KINGSLEY FREGENE grew up on the banks of the Niger River. As a young boy he was fascinated by flight. He made paper airplanes and watched in awe as sunbirds zipped through the sky.

Many years later, as an engineer, Kingsley studied how hummingbirds fly and how maple seeds, called samaras, sail on the breeze. As a seed falls from a tree, it twirls through the air. Its wing spins around and around, helping it stay up longer, fly farther, and land in a sunny spot to grow.

Kingsley decided to mimic this brilliant design. He and his team created a single-winged drone and named it the Samarai.

Today Kingsley and other engineers are investigating how animals like insects, birds, and fish move together as a group. If they can get many air vehicles to fly together, they can reduce how much energy each machine uses.

Lizard Sticky Tricks

You can really get a grip with Geckskin technology. This sticky stuff is based on a prototype that is so strong that a piece the size of your hand can stick a motorcycle to the wall.

It is made of two parts: a soft nylon that sticks like tape to a surface and a stiff woven fabric that holds the connection in place. If you try to drag the sticky pad, it won't budge, but if you pull it up and away from the surface the way a gecko peels its foot up, voilà! The adhesive comes right off.

DUNCAN IRSCHICK and ALFRED CROSBY

watched tokay geckos walk up walls and saunter across ceilings. They wanted to know this lizard's sticky tricks. Under a high-powered microscope, they observed that the gecko's toe pads were covered with thousands of tiny bristles, called setae.

Through many experiments, Duncan and Alfred explored how these setae work with the tendons in a gecko's foot. Tendons are tissues that act like super-strong rubber bands. They are flexible, which helps the gecko's foot mold to a surface. They are also stiff, which helps hold the foot firmly in place.

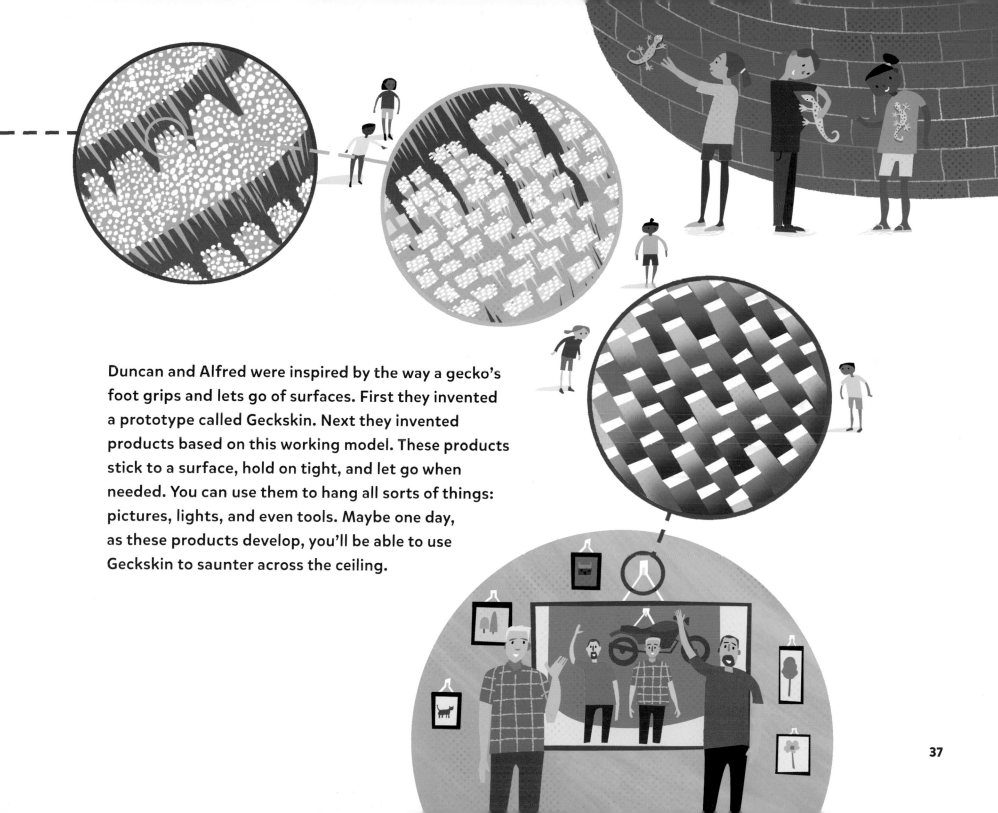

Duncan and Alfred were inspired by the way a gecko's foot grips and lets go of surfaces. First they invented a prototype called Geckskin. Next they invented products based on this working model. These products stick to a surface, hold on tight, and let go when needed. You can use them to hang all sorts of things: pictures, lights, and even tools. Maybe one day, as these products develop, you'll be able to use Geckskin to saunter across the ceiling.

It doesn't matter where you live—

in a city, on a farm, or by the sea.

Nature's secrets are waiting for you.

Wonder, investigate, and learn from the living world.
Become a mimic maker and invent something new!

More About These Mimic Makers

Mimic makers work in many different professions:

- **Architects** design buildings.

- **Botanists** are scientists who study plants.

- **Biologists** are scientists who study living things like animals, plants, and fungi.

- **Chemical engineers** design ways to safely use chemicals, materials, and energy.

- **Design engineers** develop products for people to use.

- **Electrical engineers** design and build electrical devices.

- **Material science engineers** conduct research into the properties of materials like metals and ceramics and use this information to develop products.

- **Mechanical engineers** design and build engines and machines.

- **Microbiologists** are scientists who study tiny organisms like bacteria and algae.

- **Zoologists** are scientists who study animals.

Anthony (Tony) Brennan, PhD: Research scientist, endowed professor in the materials science and engineering department at the University of Florida, founder of Sharklet Technologies.

Alfred J. Crosby, PhD: Professor in the polymer science and engineering department at the University of Massachusetts Amherst, co-inventor of Geckskin.

Frank Fish, PhD: Biologist, professor of biology at West Chester University, president of WhalePower Corporation.

Kingsley Fregene, PhD: Principal research scientist and group leader for robotics and intelligent systems at Lockheed Martin.

Duncan J. Irschick, PhD: Integrative biologist and innovator specializing in animal athletics, professor in the biology department at the University of Massachusetts Amherst, co-inventor of Geckskin and Beastcam.

Yueh-Lin (Lynn) Loo, PhD: Chemical engineer; Theodora D. '78 & William H. Walton III '74 Professor in Engineering and director of the Andlinger Center for Energy and the Environment at Princeton University.

Nakatsu Eiji: Former director of technical development at West Japan Railway Company. (Eiji's family name is Nakatsu, and his personal name is Eiji. Family names come first in Japanese culture.)

Pak Kitae: Industrial and graphic designer for Yanko Design. (Kitae's family name is Pak, and his personal name is Kitae. Family names come first in Korean culture.)

Regina Redman, PhD: Geneticist and molecular biologist; CSO and founder of Adaptive Symbiotic Technologies, Seattle; president of Symbiogenics.

Rusty Rodriguez, PhD: Microbiologist; founder and CEO of Symbiogenics; CEO of Adaptive Symbiotic Technologies, Seattle.

41

More About Biomimicry

GLOSSARY

condense: to change from a vapor or gas to a liquid

denticle: a tiny V-shaped structure that forms on a shark's skin

photosynthesis: the process by which green plants use the energy from sunlight to make food

prototype: an early, physical version of a product

samara: a seed with papery "wings" that carry it away from the tree

seta (*plural* setae): a small, stiff, hair-like structure on a plant or animal

tendon: a tissue in an animal that connects the muscle to the bone

WHAT IS BIOMIMICRY?

Mimic makers are inventors who work in the scientific field of biomimicry. *Bio* means life, and *mimicry* means copying. When you put the two words together, you get biomimicry, the process of copying life to solve problems.

Janine Benyus, a science writer, invented the word *biomimicry*. She also wrote a book for adults that reminds us nature can be our teacher. The living world knows how to run on sunlight and doesn't make trash or harmful chemicals. So when humans are struggling for ways to keep our planet cool and our air and water clean, we need to go outside, make observations, ask questions, and start looking for solutions in nature.

AUTHOR'S NOTE

I interviewed each person in this book on the phone or through email. It was both an honor and lots of fun talking with these innovators, whose inventions are helping people and changing the world. They generously shared their discoveries, patiently explained their ideas, and always said such kind and encouraging words to me about being a teacher. At the end of each interview, I asked what advice they would give to children. Do you know what they told me again and again? Don't be afraid to ask questions, don't be afraid to fail, and don't give up. That's good advice no matter how old you are! So don't be discouraged by the big challenges in the fight to keep our planet clean. Anything is possible with those wise words and nature as our guide.

How to Be a Mimic Maker

I know what you're thinking: I'm going to give you stuff to do that will turn you into a mimic maker. Guess what? You're a mimic maker right now. How? Do you think you can learn something from nature? Could nature help you solve a problem in the human world? If the answer is yes, then you're looking at the living world in a whole new way, and that's the first step.

OBSERVE

Make a Mimic Maker Journal. Take it outside and sketch what you see: a hawk circling overhead, a bending blade of grass, or leaves moving in the breeze. Write down questions you have about your sketches. Check out John Muir Laws's website for more guidance on journaling (www.johnmuirlaws.com).

CREATE

Make a 3D model based on your sketches. You could make tree bark with clay or ladybug wings with wax paper. What questions do you have when you look at your model? Write those questions in your journal. You could research the answers or ask the experts at a group like the Audubon Society (www.audubon.org). You could also explore AskNature (www.asknature.org) to learn about problems nature has already solved.

INVENT

When you make interesting discoveries (and you will, I promise), invent something useful based on your findings. You can draw your design in your journal or create it on a computer using a design program. Next build a prototype (a 3D model of your invention) and test it out, redesign and improve it, and test it again. For invention inspiration, check out the Biomimicry Institute (www.biomimicry.org) and their Youth Design Challenge.

ENGINEER

Reverse engineer an invention. Start by investigating a plant or animal you're really curious about. Do you think spinner dolphins or pitcher plants are amazing? Discover facts about them to spark your creativity. Observe their unique structures in photos and videos or in real life. What function do these structures have? What can you imagine and invent based on this new information? Sketch your invention in your journal. List the materials you need and why. If you want, you can get started with the ideas on my website (www.kristennordstrom.com).

PROBLEM-SOLVE

Mimic makers make the world a better place. So find a problem you care about and try to solve it. Don't worry if the problem seems too big or too small. The most important thing is that you want to help people and the planet we all share. Start inventing today!

Selected Bibliography

While writing this book, I interviewed the inventors and read many books on plants, animals, and biomimicry. I also read scientific articles about the inventors' research. Here are some of the most helpful resources I used:

Benyus, Janine M. *Biomimicry: Innovation Inspired by Nature*. New York: HarperCollins, 1998.

Fish, Frank E., and George V. Lauder. "Passive and Active Flow Control by Swimming Fishes and Mammals." *Annual Review of Fluid Mechanics* 38 (January 2006): 193–224.

Fregene, Kingsley, and Cortney Bolden. "Dynamics and Control of a Biomimetic Single-Wing Nano Air Vehicle." 2010 American Control Conference. June 30–July 2, 2010.

Henschel, Joh R., and Mary K. Seely. "Ecophysiology of Atmospheric Moisture in the Namib Desert." *Atmospheric Research* 87 (March 2008): 362–68.

Kim, Jong Bok, Pilnam Kim, Nicolas C. Pégard, Soong Ju Oh, Cherie R. Kagan, Jason W. Fleischer, Howard Stone, and Yueh-Lin Loo. "Wrinkles and Deep Folds as Photonic Structures in Photovoltaics." *Nature Photonics* 6 (May 2012): 327–32.

King, Daniel R., Michael D. Bartlett, Casey A. Gilman, Duncan J. Irschick, and Alfred J. Crosby. "Creating Gecko-Like Adhesives for 'Real World' Surfaces." *Advanced Materials* 26 (July 2014): 4345–51.

Kirschner, Chelsea M., and Anthony B. Brennan. "Bio-Inspired Antifouling Strategies." *Annual Review of Materials Research* 42 (August 2012): 211–29.

Mashimo, Shinya, Eiji Nakatsu, Toshiyuki Aoki, and Kazuyasu Matsuo. "Attenuation and Distortion of a Compression Wave Propagating in a High-Speed Railway Tunnel." *Transactions of the Japan Society of Mechanical Engineers Part B* 62 (January 1996): 1847–54.

Rodriguez, Rusty, and Regina Redman. "More Than 400 Million Years of Evolution and Some Plants Still Can't Make It on Their Own: Plant Stress Tolerance via Fungal Symbiosis." *Journal of Experimental Botany* 59 (March 2008): 1109–14.

Learn More!

BOOKS

General Reference

Explanatorium of Nature (DK, 2017)

Wild Buildings and Bridges: Architecture Inspired by Nature by Etta Kaner, illustrated by Carl Wiens (Kids Can Press, 2018)

Animal Features

Creature Features: Twenty-Five Animals Explain Why They Look the Way They Do by Steven Jenkins and Robin Page (HMH Books for Young Readers, 2014)

What If You Had Animal Teeth!? by Sandra Markle, illustrated by Howard McWilliam (Scholastic, 2013), and other books in the What If You Had series

Beetles

A Beetle Is Shy by Dianna Hutts Aston, illustrated by Sylvia Long (Chronicle, 2016)

The Beetle Book by Steve Jenkins (Houghton Mifflin Books for Young Readers, 2012)

Birds

Bird Watching for Kids: Bite-Sized Learning & Backyard Projects by George H. Harrison (Willow Creek, 2015)

Feathers: Not Just for Flying by Melissa Stewart, illustrated by Sarah S. Brannan (Charlesbridge, 2014)

Fungus/Microbes

Tiny Creatures: The World of Microbes by Nicola Davies, illustrated by Emily Sutton (Candlewick, 2014)

Geckos

Geckos by Katie Marsico (Scholastic, 2013)

Leaves

Exploring Leaves by Kristin Sterling (Lerner, 2012)

Trees, Leaves, and Bark by Diane L. Burns, illustrated by Linda Garrow (NorthWord, 1995)

Seeds

A Seed Is Sleepy by Dianna Hutts Aston, illustrated by Sylvia Long (Chronicle, 2007)

A Seed Is the Start by Melissa Stewart (National Geographic Kids, 2018)

Next Time You See a Maple Seed by Emily Morgan (NSTA Kids, 2014)

Sharks

Everything Sharks by Ruth A. Musgrave (National Geographic Kids, 2011)

Sharkopedia: The Complete Guide to Everything Shark by the Discovery Channel (Time Home Entertainment, 2013)

Whales

A Book About Whales by Andrea Antinori (Abrams, 2019)

Whales by Kay de Silva (CreateSpace Independent Publishing, 2015)

WEBSITES

AskNature
www.asknature.org

The Biomimicry Institute
www.biomimicry.org

The Kids' Science Challenge (Click "Teachers & Parents," select "Scientist Audio Programs," and scroll to "Bio-Inspired Design")
www.kidssciencechallenge.com

Science Buddies (Search for "biomimicry")
www.sciencebuddies.org

Science News for Students (Search for "biomimicry")
www.sciencenewsforstudents.org

The URLs listed here were accurate at publication, but websites often change. If a URL doesn't work, you can use the internet to find more information.

To Gunnar, Patrick, and Marcus. Thank you for your love and encouragement every step of the way.—K. N.

To Bobbie, Zeb, Johnny, and Bea.—P. B.

A portion of the author's profits from sales of this book will be donated to the Biomimicry Institute's Youth Design Challenge.

Photo Credits
Page 40: Photo of Anthony Brennan copyright © Jimmy Ho; photo of Alfred Crosby copyright © Jill Crosby; photo of Frank Fish courtesy of Frank Fish. Page 41: Photo of Kingsley Fregene copyright © Lockheed Martin; photo of Duncan Irschick copyright © John Solem; photo of Yueh-Lin Loo copyright © David Kelly Crow; photo of Nakatsu Eiji courtesy of Nakatsu Eiji; photo of Pak Kitae courtesy of Pak Kitae; photo of Regina Redman copyright © Rusty Rodriguez; photo of Rusty Rodriguez copyright © Sang Cho.

Published by Charlesbridge
9 Galen Street
Watertown, MA 02472
(617) 926-0329
www.charlesbridge.com

Printed in China
(hc) 10 9 8 7 6 5 4 3

Illustrations created in Photoshop from scanned pencil sketches
Display type set in Populaire by PintassilgoPrints
Text type set in Mikado by Hannes von Doehren
Color separations by Colourscan Print Co Pte Ltd, Singapore
Printed by 1010 Printing International Limited in Huizhou, Guangdong, China
Production supervision by Jennifer Most Delaney
Designed by Diane M. Earley & Jon M. Simeon

Library of Congress Cataloging-in-Publication Data
Names: Nordstrom, Kristen, author. | Boston, Paul (Illustrator).
Title: Mimic makers: biomimicry inventors inspired by nature / Kristen Nordstrom; illustrated by Paul Boston.
Description: Watertown, MA: Charlesbridge, [2021] | Includes bibliographical references. | Audience: Ages 7–10. | Summary: "In biomimicry, scientists imitate traits found in nature. An engineer shapes the nose of his bullet train like a kingfisher's beak. A scientist models her solar cell on the mighty leaf. Discover how ten inventors were inspired by animals and plants to create cutting-edge technology."—Provided by publisher.
Identifiers: LCCN 2019052338 (print) | LCCN 2019052339 (ebook) | ISBN 9781580899475 (hardcover) | ISBN 9781632898173 (ebook)
Subjects: LCSH: Biomimicry—Juvenile literature. | Inventions—Juvenile literature. | Inventors—Juvenile literature. | Technological innovations—Juvenile literature. | Nature—Miscellanea—Juvenile literature.
Classification: LCC QP517.B56 N67 2021 (print) | LCC QP517.B56 (ebook) | DDC 610.28—dc23
LC record available at https://lccn.loc.gov/2019052338
LC ebook record available at https://lccn.loc.gov/2019052339